UGLY LOVE
(Notes from the Negro Side of the Moon)

EARL BRAGGS

Winter Soup Bowl Chapbook
2016 Selection 1 of 2   CB1

C&R Press
Conscious & Responsible
www.crpress.org

For special discounted bulk purchases please contact:
C&R Press sales@crpress.org

UGLY LOVE
(Notes from the Negro Side of the Moon)

Black on Black crime, as you may know, is random niggers

shooting and robbing and killing other random niggers.

A white collar crime, wide as Wall Street, white as a white

Oxford white shirt, tucked perfectly. Black on Black crime,

a corporate American investment, business as usual, not

a crime at press time. Weekend niggers on the evening news,

strung–out straight, constitutional, like a rope dangling

from the thin, white arms of a psychological lynching tree.

If only we'd arrived without the history of difficult music.

Jazz. If only Charles Darwin had explained the evolution

of strange fruit. Lady Day sings the blues, Billy Holiday

wearing a white carnation in her hair, circa 1936. Jazz.

Strange fruit, a white collar crime, which is not a crime

as is black on black crime, "bottom line" designed to keep

the business side of prison life deep in the "Black" cash–

flow. Poverty, welfare population projected sky high. Negro

cash–flow. Mr. and Mrs. Dow Jones needs Negroeconomics.

Nasdaq, hedge funds. New York City niggers, New York City

Stock Exchange, commodities. Stock so low it can only go up.

Negro stock, a share of drop–straight–dead–right–now nigger

Money, Mississippi Negro stock. Cock the trigger nigger,

you're the one who's being robbed blind by a blind man.

It's a set–up, set up like a stage. Hollywood is real good

at tricking niggers into believing they can fly like a kite,

like Superman. The great escape, no cape required, walk

straight off the edge of a cliff. If only we'd arrived without

the history of difficult music. Jazz. But somehow the art of

the art history of slavery taught niggers how to soar at night,

in the dark, by mistake. Take Miles Dewey Davis, LIVE

at the BLACKHAWK, San Francisco, 1957, soaring, starless,

'cross a sky full of unlit lamp lights with no need of "no"

Batman cape, just a horn section snatching stars anyway,

all the way from the other side of the Negro side of the moon,

hypnotizing an audience, mostly white. Miles Dewey Davis,

playing solo, back to the people, mostly white. Why, when

asked, said, "Hell, they came to see me, I didn't come to see

them." Miles Dewey Davis hypnotizing the construction of

ugly love conversations, talking to, away from and about

the ins and the only way out for a Negro in America. Miles

ahead, Miles behind, running down the voodoo, running

down the naked, unabashed truth from a Hollywood point

of view. Trumpeted moon, watered down blue, Miles Dewey

Davis muffled down deep in transitional tragic Negro music,

real dark–black magic music, practicing the ability to slide

artfully in, then out of tempo in stereo, playing that spaced–out

space between nigger–rated notes of street Negro sheet music all the way down there where Wall Street crosses Mr. James

Madison Avenue. Benjamin Franklin's picture scattered 'cross

the stock market trading room floor. The whole wide world

waiting for a closing bell to ring. Swing low South Carolina

basket making sweet grass people and all the Negro has ever

been allowed to do is sing beautifully at that intersection where

Nigger Street crosses Nigger Avenue crosses Niggerhead Road.

If only we'd arrived without the history of difficult music. Jazz.

American needs Negroeconomics just as much, but not more

than America needs to sing praises to her Negro children

every Sunday morning. You cannot sit still, America. Sunday

morning African–American–Negro–nigger gospel church music.

Like angles flying towards Heaven, the voice of Negroes sing

like "no tomorrow" is tomorrow morning's moment's notice,

all dressed up. Sam Cooke wearing James Brown shoes. Church

people we are, always have been. Not a doubt to even talk about.

Negroes love sermons that drive up in big pretty Cadillacs, big

enough so you and everybody else knows the unacknowledged

dark—dark shadowed black voodoo power of Black Power people.

Look at any Sunday morning Black church parking lot near you.

Mr. General Motors CEO loves niggers because niggers invented

Cadillacs and a Coupe de Ville—Eldorado before the idea of. But

now you tell to me this, if you will. What is the price of ugly love?

The American Negro, the only people on the planet who can be

dead—flat broke and still have a pocket full of money. The complete,

earned essence of black magic. Flat—out broke and not quite broke

simultaneously. Simultaneous, ingenious niggers, broke and not

all at the same time, playing that clever—fox space between street—

notes, smooth as fresh corn silk soul. Voodoo economics. Goat head

on a cheese platter. Hog head cheese on a supper table. Monday

evening neckbones, Tuesday morning pig's feet. Rastafarian root

doctors working turnip roots on the backdoor steps of Carolina

like the tick–tock–tick workings of the hands of a lottery clock.
Negro–nigger stock, not a question but here's a real good inquiry.

What would America be without the beautiful black beauty of
her Negro people? What exact non–color would our flag want not

to be? You see, it's about the price of Alabama city bus fare, yellow
cab fare, subway token fare, a train, American airline ticket–flight

to a new nice place the new nice niggers (some say as early as 1621)
did not want to go. It takes an American "rocket scientist" not to

acknowledge the art history of realizing that "Designing a Negro
Cadillac" for all Americans is, was and then the most lucrative

capital Ad–venture in the history of General Motors. Ford Motors
too, if you know your own art history. Chief Financial Officers love

niggers. Negroeconomics. The spending power of the American Negro
is greater than and/or equal to that of Canada combined with Mexico.

Now, that doesn't even begin to figure into the musical financial
funeral arrangements of that John Lee Hooker style of illegal nigger–

economics. Zoot, overly long, voodoo suits, pretty platinum pocket

watches on a fake gold chain. Dressed—up niggers going to church

to worship a hand—me—down, secondhand Jesus Christ, some say

as early as 1621. The religiosity of cheap "rhetorics" and politics.

But truth be truly told, the American Negro cannot afford not to

believe in the God given the moment Africans stepped on the boat.

Cock the trigger nigger, you're the one who's getting robbed

blind by a blind man with the need of "no" seeing—eye bulldog

to see nigger stock on SALE at the corner of Independence Street

and Madison Avenue. Voodoo economics, the art history of *Soul*

on Ice, Eldridge Cleaver's letters from prison mailed to Angela

Yvonne Davis, George Jackson, and his little brother Jonathan,

just 17, a judge, a rope, and a shotgun. A revolution televised

with too many unanswered, definitive question marks. What

is the SALE price of ugly love? Angela Y. Davis asked the judge.

Angela Y. Davis, a fired philosophy professor, fired point blank

for teaching rhetoric–not–composition at the prestigious University
of California at Los Angeles. Angela Yvonne Davis afro–picked

the biggest, the bushiest, the most beautiful, the bushiest, the most
natural, the "baddest" afro the black and white photograph people

living nice and un–nice on this side of F. Scott Fitzgerald's paradise
pond would ever, themselves, come to know. The Roaring Twenties

roared again, but loud as an African lion in the H. Rap Brown 1960s
America. The 1960s, a decade defined by hair, a revolutionary afro.

Angela Y. Davis' African hair–do was so "bad" and bushy, rightly
one might go as far as to say there would have been no roaring 1960s

without Angela Y. Davis' afro bushed-out preaching the politics of
a red, black and green revolution. Soul Sister Angela Yvonne Davis

standing on the racist jail house steps of the racist Marin County
Court House talking about *If They Come in the Morning*, I won't

be good but I will be ready unlike Fred Hampton, surprised by
his sleep when the nigger–killers came to Chicago to wake him up

that same morning in Oakland, California, Huey P. Newton
was handing out Black Panthers style free breakfasts. Angela Y.

Davis fired for flame–torch throwing the school house down
with the rhetoric of revolution. Angela Y. Davis fired point

blank like a gunshot in 1969 by none other than the Honorable
Ronald Wilson Reagan, the same Mr. Ronald Wilson Reagan,

the 40th US President but then the Hollywood star Governor
of the great state of CA. Somebody, everybody left out the I.

Angela Yvonne Davis barred from school teaching for teaching
Black Panther Philosophy in a UCLA philosophy class. Angela

Y. Davis, properly dismissed to the Negro side of the moon for
listening to Miles Davis, flat laying down deep, out, on the top of

In a Silent Way, blowing Moon Dreams like a baby boy blowing
bubbles. Miles Dewey Davis and a trumpet, some cool nights

he called Sally. Miles Dewey Davis and Miss Sally Mae blowing
up a gale force wind disguised as a dancing hurricane, dancing

down into the storm at the center of the center of an eye—circle of

voodoo girls, miles away from himself and any and everyone else.

Miles bent over damn—near backwards, blowing that trumpet

at the end of the world, straight up in the night sky like Gabriel.

Birth of the Cool, the year of our Lord, 1949. Miles Dewey

Davis hunting down the boogie man and the reggae boogie

woman too, as in also in, the other dark corner, just as cool,

weighing in at just over 200 lbs., fighting out of Rocky Mount,

North Carolina, Thelonious Sphere Monk Junior, cascading

piano keys like pocket change, like lukewarm clear water,

banging a piano like he's wearing a hat with a boxing glove.

What is the price of ugly love? she asked. Angela Y. Davis.

The audience, mostly white, was an uproar. They loved Monk

Junior and John Coltrane and Art Blakey and Dizzy Gillespie.

The great debate never was a debate. Get the story straight.

No need to debate the necessary, no contrary. The truth. No

question, no dispute here in the name of the Father, the Son, and the Holy Spirit. The great debate never was a debate.

Every white American born in the United States of America loves, loves Negro music, but... What is the price of ugly love?

she asked. Angela Yvonne Davis, Queen Sister of a Revolution. Super "Bad" as in super bold, bold as in love with her own afro

picked, made for a made–for–television (Red, Black and Green) revolution, yet now, no more than a TV time–out commercial

break. We asked that you, "Do not make the fatal mistake of hearing exactly what you listen to behind those Foster Grants.

No big or small surprise, so dark not even God can see your eyes reflecting Negroes, niggers and such. Every Negro in America

knows Miles poured a whole bucket full of voodoo into an already full bucket full of Bitch's Brew. That cotton–seed–nigger music you

love, American, is laced. The voodoo truth. Nigger–Zen. Next of kin, we are. America loves Negroes. If only we'd arrived without

the history of... But I will not tip my hat to empty hearted love?
The Book of Hats tells us that Booker Taliaferro Washington said,

"The first thing the newly freed slave thought about was a name
and the second was a hat." Dignity. Dignity from digging in dirt,

Mississippi delta black, rich, fertile dirt dignity, the people wanted.
The Negro wanted the spirit of America to take her sunglasses off.

But the spirit of America was and is still blind as Blind Lemon
Jefferson, 1893. America, in her defense, sells, buys, and rents

more sunglasses and winter weather sun shades than any other
country in the universe. Worse, America is with her suburban

blue eyes "Nice work if you can get it" Philosophy and Religion
course laid out like a "Masters" Augusta, Georgia golf course.

No great need or urgency to see reality. Eventually a golf ball
will find a hole in one nigger's socks. Only the consequences of

CNN Headline News makes the news. Black on black crime
is not a crime at press time, re–pressed, sadly told, dangling

like rope from the arms of a psychological lynching tree.

Branches of which, visible from the dark side of the moon.

"Soon" is still a natural science that the Negro in America

is forced to believe because America refuses to acknowledge

the black, natural black beauty of being born black in America.

If only we'd arrived without the history of difficult music. Jazz.

Andrew Carnegie built the Carnegie Library and Carnegie Hall,

but Negroes built America. Slavery was a superbly good deal

with a zero percent interest rate to pay–back loan interest rate.

America could not wait to spend–up all that cotton seed oil.

America, land of no castles to speak not of, but a house of many

mansions. America has too much and too–plenty of everything.

Mix that with two–penny niggers and you get the Soul of what

you get, a voice so beautiful, it sings only to the constellations.

Columbia Records knows, exactly, what I am talking about.

Ask the CFO if you want to know who Whitney Houston really is.

And why did it take a white–boy British Invasion, the Beatles,

the Rolling Stones, the Kinks, the Troggs, the Who to tell to you,

America, that rock 'n roll has a slave ship narrative in her Soul.

There's nothing but cotton seed oil in the history of rock 'n roll.

John Lennon was living in New York City when he told the FBI,

"You don't like me because I love nigger music..." Deportation

papers filed. The United States of America vs. John Winston Lennon.

Guilty for being a white boy, acknowledging the voice of black beauty.

Sargent Pepper's Lonely Heart Club Band like Elvis dug up that

Little Richard, Chuck Berry music from the dirt of difficult times.

If only we'd arrived without the history of difficult music. Jazz.

We, the Negro of America, do solemnly swear that we were born

out on the limbs of a lynching tree on the other side of the moon

over America in the back seat of a jazzed up and out blue blues bus.

We grew up hat–dancing on Bourbon Street and Beale Street. Oh,

If Beale Street Could Talk is what James Baldwin said. Hat People.

Hat–wearing people, we are because Negroes are the only people
on the planet whose hair grows straight up to meet the morning sun.

A hat gives hair grease a certain kind of velvet smooth voodooness.
The black magic of Madame C. J. Walker knows exactly in dollars

and much larger bills. Born Sarah Breedlove in dirt Delta, LA
in, some say, 1867, made million dollars selling green pomade

hair grease to New York City Negroes before the mail order catalog
was mail ordered. Negroeconomics sleeping with Mrs. Sears and

Roebuck. The first female self–made millionaire in the history of...
Madam C. J. Walker knows, but every Sunday morning, every day,

Negro church ladies know the biology of slavery far better than any
of us. Every Easter morning, they come and go to church wearing

Queen sized hats. They call their Sunday–church–hats crowns.
An impresario of hats so big you can't see the preacher preaching

to a Negro gospel choir on any Sunday morning is a royal place to be
not only in Money, Mississippi, if you asks me about the hair grease

in Robert Johnson's crosshair blues. Robert Johnson slapping
that guitar, slapping it like a woman he "done clean" forgot how

to love. *I Believe I'll Dust My Broom* Blues. Let me finish tying up
my shoes blues. Robert Johnson slapping between nights that

rained gunshots hot as star light on a dead-dark–nigger moonless–
moon night. Robert Johnson, hurricane–tornado Negro thunder,

rain. Wet gun smoke power blues. The smell of love never was
a question mark meant. Shot by mistake. What is the SALE price

of ugly love? Issue an arrest warrant for my arrest. I am guilty,
no reasonable doubt. I stole the world when you weren't looking.

I am a nigger, a Negro, colored, an African–American just like–
like American planned for me to be. Lunatic politics and tricks.

No astrological need for any scientific double–blind investigation.
Trigger–niggernometry. Black on Black crime is not a crime. It's

a strategy to put me in between me and me so I only see in double
motion. Like smoke–lotion, slavery was and is a well–oiled machine.

Gangs do what gangs do, kill other gangs and us. Webster defines
Gang: Six or five or seven or just one black–Negro–niggers standing

on a dark street corner, leaning sideways up against a light post,
a street sign, with nothing else to do but scare the living shit out

of each and every last page in the book of a White Science Book.
Naturally, people afraid of niggers, naturally, smile more often,

and naturally when the white history of white America tells
the reverse side of the story of our lunar landing, America

starts every time with this line: Bouncing like a Myrtle Beach,
South Carolina beach ball, Neil Armstrong planted two flags,

one with thirteen stars and two bars of candy on the Negro side
of the moon, easy as pie, like placing the Confederate Battle Flag

on one side of the George Washington, DC US Capitol dome.
"Houston, we have a problem, there's niggers already up here."

"How do you copy, Houston? Did you hear what I said, Houston?"
"Houston we have a problem, there's niggers already up here."

Lunatic Street is on Main Street, but it would not be if scientists

could ever get it straight and stop shooting niggers by mistake

behind the face of a 2nd Amendment meant not for niggers, but

exclusively for un–niggers. Want to change the 2nd Amendment.

Let a bunch of niggers, all over America, go down to Lincoln

National Park packing heat, waving, wearing pistols like cowboys,

like John Wayne facing down Clint Eastwood on the main stage

in Hollywood. It's good, but most likely, it will not be. You see

the NRA would cry if America would ask "Why" without being

drunk, under the influence of rose–tinted dark blue sunglass lens.

Oh the sweet, dirt, smell of regret for leaving out the details

of a rose, a Confederate Rose knows the exact exactness of love,

a nigger, even as it changes colors from white to pink to deep

red rose, a perennial, shrubby, treelike unlike, but just like

a lynch. It behaves smooth like a perennial, comes back yearly,

knotted like a rope, proving beyond no doubt, only a shadow

of "Why" America wears the dead–of–night darkest, the most

expensive sun glasses in the universe, designed to hide niggers

from the world. A trick for a lunatic, a grand scheme designed,

designed executively by the Polo fragrances of Calvin Klein

and Frankenstein. Sunglasses worn not only when America

goes to see Walt Disney's world or the ski mountains of Vale,

Colorado. America wears her sunglasses black like night, no

insight, black as the dark side of a full moon eclipse. America,

blind as Blind Lemon Jefferson circa before and after 1921.

America the Beautiful, land of the blind. Blind as a baseball

bat slung all the way out into center field after she strikes out

walking towards black beauty thwarted by ugly love, walking

'til the grass turns green and starts to grow money on trees.

The Negro economic impact of cotton seed oil lubricates well

and good in Hollywood. America, a superstar on the world's stage,

and she wears her dark sunglasses as well as any Oscar nominee.

Still the United States flat–out refuses the lyrics of "Matchbox Blues,"
Robert Johnson burning a hole in the pockets of America's favorite

pastime, counting niggers on the nightly news, counting college
football niggers on Saturday, counting NFL niggers on Sunday

after church. What would America be without her Negro people?
What is the price of ugly love? How much does a pair of sunglasses

really cost? White crosses are still burning in America. Visions of
a Confederate rose–colored Saturday night lynch party circa 1936.

Photograph in black and white: Black man hanging from a tree.
Same photograph: An ordinary white township of ordinary white

families witnessing like church, standing back, un–proper aesthetic
distance, watching this nigger, he not she, dangle from the sky,

watching this nigger like watching a good ol' western cowboy flick.
Buttered up popcorn, I don't know or care. But it appears, solemnly,

to me that they were having a good time watching that nigger dance
like no tomorrow, no yesterday played out and plotted in red paint.

Fear and quilted guilt carved out then sewn into the fabric of falsity,
a quilt, too warm for the weather, stitched cross stripes, rebel–state

plaid, a kilt. Tilt the telescope, listen to the way the moon hides
her side with eyes disguised in the wax and wane of shotgun love

over rice with gunshot rain. Wet but not from tears. Odd years
that count themselves without redemption. The tried and true

nature of a slave auction is a terrible wonderful love affair. Dark
brown people, darker than dark blue, black as Miles Dewey Davis

bought and sold on an open air market like lilacs and daffodils.
Guaranteed to please. If you've always wanted the intoxicating scent

of a daffodil nigger in your garden, but don't think you have room,
take a look at this here pretty nigger girl. Nile River black, beautiful,

she flows just as, face shaped like the moon, eyes that wakeup stars.
Nigger girl, seventeen at most, her pink perfume body blooms heavily

in May and, after a short rest, flowers again intermittently until fall.
Lilacs, daffodils, niggers without names. *Nobody Knows My Name,*

James Baldwin said. Charming she is, she gives a Negro parade of
color for patio containers, pathways, intimate spaces, clamped places.

Upright, her bushy form reaches just 5 and a half feet. Shipped
straight up to your front door in a ship, next—day—same—day delivery.

The United States Postal Service, rain, sleet, or snow, the show must go
on in America. A boat load of niggers in a two quart crockpot delivered

at the proper time for planting season. Recommended for planting zones
anywhere between Money, Mississippi to Money, Mississippi. Burning

ink signs a nigger burning deal in steel. The ink does not want to dry.
Slave auction, Market Street, lilacs, daffodils and us born out on a limb,

sold to the lowest bidder if the highest bidder didn't show up that day.
Christopher Columbus didn't discover America, America discovered

the Cherokee, the Chickasaw, the Algonquian, the Mississippian,
the Chappaquiddick, the Seneca, the Shawnee, the Iroquois, the Creek,

the Chippewa, the Comanche and then, and then America discovered
niggers in the bottom of a boat load. Amistad, Amistad where art thou

then and now. 1839 mutiny aboard La Amistad. La Amistad means

friendship in Spanish. La Amistad means too many people wearing

sun glasses in the rain in English. What is the price of ugly love?

Christopher Columbus didn't discover America, America discovered

Pocahontas sitting next to Sitting Bull, Geronimo, New Mexico

and a patch of dirt brown niggers dancing and singing in the dark

on the dark side of a full moon wearing silver handcuff jewelry

bracelets. Leg shackles optional, the optimum optical illusion.

Now you see, now you don't see that nigger dangling, dancing

from the shadows of a strange fruit tree, but still just as sweet

as homemade Southern sweet ice tea. Shade filtered light blocks

the blessed black beauty of everydayness, Negro side of the moon.

Black on Black crime was a wonderfully marvelous invention,

looking out from the perspective of the ugly. Me, I was voted

the ugliest boy on the school bus because I was the only Negro

on the school bus. I even got the school bus driver's vote. Note

the angle and slant of a school bus driving chair. Look at the way
half–light appears on half–nights like this. Blues and radio jazz.

1969 was a terribly wonderful, marvelous year. Neil Armstrong
walked on the moon and me kicked out of high school for inciting

a race riot. Pender County, NC, the Board of Education declared
that I was unfit because my pants didn't fit my ass like a white boy.

Furthermore and therefore, there will be no further questions
when there had never been any questions at all to speak not of

anyway. 1969 was a marketable year. Stock markets love the moon.
America planted an American apple pie flag tree on the side we see,

but the side that sees us when we are not looking looks a lot like
the white horse ghost of Robert E. Lee, tall in the saddle, white hat,

white hair, white beard, white Southern breeze, a rebel flag.
Robert E. Lee decked out in gray, wearing sunglasses in the rain.

Tall in the saddle as Richmond, Virginia, Robert E. Lee staring
at me and the trash truck people with mops who now live outside

of, on the outskirts of ugly love, down here where a lynched nigger photograph is as ordinary as the time of day in Money, Mississippi.

Black people are broke. The Native Americans are broke, but also the Native American spirit is broken into reservation sized pieces.

Slavery could not break the African spirit. All is well on that front. Black people are broke because Negroes worked for 300 years

and did not get paid and all white America can say is "Them niggers are unemployed because them niggers don't wanna work."

The history of living a lie is the history of wearing dark sunglasses in the rain. But America doesn't really want to see the dark beauty

of the night, her own dark skinned children inherited from cotton fields, rice fields, indigo fields, salvation fields of tobacco juice dirt.

John D. Rockefeller built Rockefeller Center, built the Rockefeller Foundation, built the Rockefeller Plaza from the ground up, but

the foundation of the United States of America was built brick by brick by brick by brick—brick—brick by the American Negro.

There is no discernible difference between Standard Oil and

cotton seed oil. Oil is Oil and a nigger is a nigger in America.

And it is projected to stay precisely that way until America stops

putting dark sunglasses on to drive through a blinding rain storm.

America the Beautiful would not be America the Beautiful,

if at all she is, without the beauty of her black biological kin,

the beautifully bright grin of her Negroes people. Who knows

what America would look like all covered in white like a sheet

covering the face of no promise whatsoever. Dirty third-day

snow. We only know that the great debate never was a debate.

Look at the other Book of Revelation and you will see "Birth of

a Nation," a good movie because it depicted the real Civil War

where the ones who won the war are the very same ones who lost

the war. Ulysses Simpson Grant ain't nothing these days but a page

down-loaded to nothing while Robert Edward Lee is in Richmond

up upon a horse, tall in the saddle, wearing sunglasses in the rain,

towering over the unsacred science of slavery, 1863. "Statued" high
upon a horse, General Robert E. Lee calm as a Greek god in Rome.

Export the Natives to Oklahoma, import a boat load of Africans.
Refer to the former as savages, the latter as niggers. Take the state

of Mexico and rename it New Mexico, California, Arizona, Texas.
Sam Houston, Andrew Jackson, Davy Crockett like the pocket knife

of Daniel Boone cutting the heart out of harvested Negro love of
America. Phillis Wheatley, the first black poet in America to publish

a book, wrote a poem to George Washington, *His Excellency General
Washington* in 1775. Wheatley born in West Africa, sold into slavery

at age seven. "Four score and seven years ago our fathers brought
forth." The Negro has always sang jazz from the dark spaces of empty

rooms. But Negro–nigger vote count seems not to know how to count
the numbers of janitor positions sweeping up dirt in the school house

hallways of America, too many still all Black. Responsible, they say,
for Black on Black crime. Responsible, they say, for the overwhelming

Black population of prison count, now you just count the under–
whelming numbers of a college degree. We, me and Brown vs the

Board of Education lost the civil War in 1954. Miss Rosa Louise Parks
is still standing, waiting for a white man to get up and let her sit

down yesterday in Montgomery, Alabama. Reverend Martin Luther
King Jr. is still standing on the steps of Abraham Lincoln, still

marching in Memphis for the garbage collectors of America. Mal-
colm is still crossing out his last name with an X. Medgar Evers is

still asleep in ditch on the side of the road in Jackson, Mississippi.
Miss Fannie Lou Hamer is still in Washington, DC yelling at LBJ and

"Lady Bird," still trying to cast a vote in Sunflower County, Mississip-
pi. Yes, things have changed, but they have not. A nigger is still a

nigger in America. And yes, America has elected a beautiful Black
First Family. And yes, we now have "our" first president. And yes

Brother Barack was born with us on the Negro side of the moon.
 And yes, also he knows the roads to Harvard, to Yale, but a nigger

is still a nigger in America, mopping, sweeping, cleaning, pick-

ing up trash on non–trash pickup days. Blind as Blind Lemon

Jefferson, America can't see simply because she does not want

to see the ebony black beauty of her Negro people. What would

America be without her plenty of everything, her sky–tall scrapers

scraping up against the very top of a nigger–built Heaven. How

can the voice of America sound of love without Aretha Franklin,

the Queen of Soul and who told you, American, what America

would be without Cassius Clay and Muhammad Ali, without Jesse

in 1936, without Jackie's number 42, without Sally?Some nights

Miles played her just like that, a woman he was trying to figure

out how to love. Miles Dewey Davis, a brother with a pocket

knife and a hat–wearing–Negro––nigger lean? I mean America

needs Angela Yvonne Davis and her "bad" afro. America knows

just as I know there would be no America without the beauty of

her Negro people triggeredin niggernometry, fictitiously normal.

Life sold by the day, a hard mule–wagon ride.

American as pie, just a slice, the price of ugly love.

OTHER C&R PRESS TITLES 2016-2017

NOVEL
That Man in Our Lives by Xu Xi
Spectrum by Martin Ott
A History of the Cat In Nine Chapters or Less by Anis Shivani

SHORT FICTION
The Protester Has Been Released by Janet Sarbanes
Medittions on the Mother Tongue by An Tran

ESSAY
Immigration Essays by Sybil Baker
Je Suis L'Autre: Essays and Interrogations by Kristina Marie Darling

POETRY
Free Boat by John Reed
The Couple Who Fell to Earth by Michelle Bitting
Tall as You are Tall Between Them by Annie Christain
Les Fauves by Narabara Crooker
Imagine Not Drowning by Kelli Allen

ANTHOLOGY
Aliens, Cyborgs, Zombies and the Ongoing Apocalypse:
Sci-Fi Poems of the 21st Century and Beyond
by Travis Denton & Katie Chaple

www.ingramcontent.com/pod-product-compliance
Lightning Source LLC
Chambersburg PA
CBHW032107040426
42449CB00007B/1211